# RELIGIOUS RESOURCES

IN

# AMERICAN LIBRARIES

AND

# HISTORICAL ASSOCIATIONS

## Dr. Charles Dickson

HERITAGE BOOKS
2013

# HERITAGE BOOKS

### AN IMPRINT OF HERITAGE BOOKS, INC.

## Books, CDs, and more—Worldwide

For our listing of thousands of titles see our website
at
www.HeritageBooks.com

Published 2013 by
HERITAGE BOOKS, INC.
Publishing Division
5810 Ruatan Street
Berwyn Heights, Md. 20740

Heritage Books by the author:
*Religious Resources in American Libraries and Historical Associations*
*Scandinavian-American Genealogical Resources*

International Standard Book Numbers
Paperbound: 978-0-7884-5485-1
Clothbound: 978-0-7884-6860-5

# PREFACE

The United States is easily the most religiously diverse nation in the world and perhaps in the history of the world. Immigrant groups coming from every nook and cranny of the globe have arrived on her shores bringing with them their distinct religious traditions.

The following work represents an attempt to produce a quick reference to the multitude of resources that are available on religious groups in American libraries and historical associations. While many individual congregations maintain libraries no attempt has been made to include them in the listing, but rather to focus on the wider picture of state, area, or regional organizations.

This work makes no claim to be an exhaustive source of information but hopefully will serve as a catalyst that will encourage researchers to probe for additional historical data and insights.

Charles Dickson
Hickory, North Carolina
January 2013

## THE AUTHOR

Dr. Dickson is an instructor at Catawba Valley
Community College in Hickory, North Carolina and
is also an ordained minister.

He has authored more than 500 articles and ten
previous books including one for Heritage titled SCANDINAVIAN AMERICAN GENEALOGICAL RESOURCES.

It is his hope that this little handbook will
provide a catalyst for historical research into
American religious groups.

# TABLE OF CONTENTS

Preface

The Author

TABLE OF CONTENTS (cont.)

Bibliographic Resources

# ADVENTIST

Adventists began in America in the 19th century under
the leadership of William Miller of Low Hampton, New
York.There are numerous branches of Adventists inclu-
ding the Seventh-Day Adventist,the Advent Christian
Church,and the Primitive Advent Christian Church.
Adventists total about 600,000 members in the U.S.

Oakwood College  Dyke Library  Huntsville,Alabama
   35896  Tel 256-726-7246  Fax 256-726-7409
   Significant collection of Adventist Black History

Pacific Union University  One Angwin Avenue  Angwin,
   Calif. 94508  Tel 707-965-6242  Fax 707-965-6504
   Web. www.library.puc.edu

Loma Linda University  11072 Anderson St.  Loma Linda,
   Calif.  92350  Tel 909-553-4581  Fax 909-558-4188
   Web www.llu.edu/llu/library  Large Seventh-Day
   Adventist historical collection.

Adventist Library  Aurora College  347 S. Gladstone
   Aurora,Illinois  60506  Tel 630-844-5437  Fax  630-
   844-3848  Web www.aurora.edu/library

Seveth-Day Adventist General Conference  Rebok Memorial
   Library  12501 Columbia Pike  Silver Spring,Maryland
   20914  Tel 301-680-6495  Fax  301-680-6090

Columbia Union College  7600 Flower Ave  Takima Park,
   Md. 20912  Tel 301-891-4217  Fax  301-891-4218
   Web www.cuc.edu/library

Carter Library Berkshire Christian College  Lenox,Mass.
   01240  Tel 413-637-0838  Advent Christ Church archives

Atlantic Union College  338 Main St.  Lancaster,Mass.01561
   Tel 978-388-2450  Fax 978-368-2456  Web. www.library.
   atlantic.edu

Andrews University Library  1400 Camous Dr.  Berrien
   Springs,Mich 49104  Tel 616-471-3264  Fax 616-471-6166
   Web www.andrews.edu/library

Southern Adventist University  Collegedale,Tenn. 37315
   Tel 423-238-2788  Fax 423-238-3009  Web www.library.
   southern.edu  Adventist publications archives.

3

# BAPTIST

Baptist history in America dates back to 1631 when
Roger Williams came to Rhode Island and shortly thereafter established a Baptist church in Providence. From
these beginnings Baptists have grown to become the
largest Protestant denomination in the U.S. having
about 28 million members in nearly 100,000 congregations.

There are 27 different Baptist groups with the largest
being the Southern Baptist Convention whose strength is
in the southern U.S. and the American Baptist Church
whose membership is primarily in northern states. There
are also several large African-American Baptist groups
plus some whose roots are in Swedish and German immigrant
groups

Samford University Library   800 Lakeshore Dr. Birmingham
    Alabama 35229   Tel 205-726-2748   Fax 205-726-4009
    Web  www.samford.edu/library

Arkansas Baptist College Library  1600 Bishop Street
    Little Rock,Arkansas 722202   Tel 501-244-5109
    Fax 501-244-5102

Central Baptist College  Cobb Library  1500 College Ave.
    Conway,Arkansas 72032   Tel 501-329-6872   Fax 501-729-
    2941   Web  www.cbc.edu

California Baptist University Library  8432 Magnolia Ave.
    Riverside,Cal. 92504   Tel 909-343-4228  Fax 909-343-
    4523   Web www.calbaptist.edu/library Baptist history
    in California

Stetson University Library  421 N. Woodland Blvd  Deland,
    Florida 32720   Tel 386-822-7175  Fax 386-740-3626
    Archives of Florida Baptist history

Mercer University Library  1021 Georgia Ave. Macon,Georgia
    31201   Tel 478-301-2612   Fax 478-301-2284   Web www.
    library.law.mercer.edu   Georgia Baptist hist. collection

Northern Baptist Theological Seminary  660 E. Butterfield
    Rd.  Lombard,Illinois 60148   Tel 630-620-2104   Fax 630
    620-2170 Web  www.seminary.edu

Central Baptist Theological Seminary  2915 Minnesota
Ave  Kansas City, Mo. 66102  Tel 816-414-3729  Fax
816-414-3728  Web  www.cbts.edu

Southern Baptist Theological Seminary  2825 Lexington
Rd. Louisville, Ky 40280  Tel 502-897-4807  Fax 502
897-4600  Web www.sbts.edu  Southern Baptist collection.

New Orleans Baptist Theological Seminary 4110 Seminary Pl.
New Orleans,La. 70126  Tel 504-816-8018  Fax 504-816-
8429  Web  www.nobts.edu

Andover Newton Theological Seminary  169 Herrick Road
Newton Center,Mass  02459  Tel 617-831-2415  Fax 617-
831-1643  Web  www.library.ants.edu  New England
Baptist history

Bethel Theological Seminary Library  3949 Bethel Drive
St. Paul,Minnesota  55112  Tel 651-638-6184  Fax 651
-638-6006 Web.  www.bethel.edu/seminary  National
records of Swedish Baptists in America

Southwestern Baptist University Library  1600 University
Ave.  Bolivar,Mo. 65613  Tel 417-328-1604  Fax 617-
328-1652 Web  www.falcon.sbumv.edu/library  Has the
Butler Baptist Heritage Collection

American Baptist-Samuel Colgate History Library  1106
S. Goodman St.  Rochester,NY 14830 Tel 585-340-9402
Fax 585-340-9403  Web  www.crds.edu/abhs  Has Danish
and Norwegian Baptist General Conference records

Southeastern Baptist Theological Seminary Library  114
N. Wingate St. Wake Forest,NC 27587  Tel 919-556-3104
Fax 919-863-8150  Web.  www.library.sebts.edu
Has North Carolina Baptist history collection

Oklahoma Baptist University Library  506 W. University
Shawnee,Okla  74801  Tel 405-878-2269  Fax 405-878-2256
Web  www.okbu.edu/library

Linfield College Library  900 S. Baker St.  McMinnville,
Oregon 97128  Tel 503-883-2517  Fax 503-883-2566
Web  www.linfield.edu/library

Furman University Library 3300 Poinsett Hwy
Greenville,S.C. 29613 Tel 864-294-2190 Fax 864
294-3004 Web www.library.furman.edu

North American Baptist Seminary Library 1525 S. Grange
Ave Sioux Falls,South Dakota 57105 Tel 605-336-6585
Fax 605-335-9090 Web www.nabs.edu Contains North
American Baptist Archives

Free Will Baptist Bible College 3650 W. 2nd Avenue
Nashville,Tenn. 37205 Tel 615-844-5274 Fax 615-
229-6028 Web www.fwbbc.edu Contains archives
of the Free Will Baptists in America

Southern Baptist Historical Library and Archives 902
Commerce St. Nashville,Tenn 37203 Tel 615-244-0344
Fax 615-782-4821

Houston Baptist University Moody Memorial Library 7502
Fondren Road Houston,Texas 77074 Tel 281-649-3435
Fax 281-649-3489 Web www.hbu.edu/library

Baylor University Library 1312 S. Third St Waco,Texas
76798 Tel 254-710-2112 Fax 254-710-1710 Web
www.baylor.edu/library

William Jewell College 500 College Hill Liberty,
Missouri 64068 Tel 816-415-7609 Fax 816-415-
5021 Web www.campus.jewell.edu/academics Has
some archives of the Baptist churches

Vorginia Baptist Historical Society Library P.O. Box
34 Richmond,Virginia 23173 Tel 804-289-8434

# BRETHREN

Brethren churvhes have their roots in Germany as a
branch OF THE Reformed Protestant movement. They have
a long history in America dating from the 1700s and
are present in eight bodies with about 300,000 members.
These groups include Church of the Brethren,Plymouth
Brethren,and the United Brethren.

University of LaVerne 2040 Third St. La Verne,Calif.
91750 Tel 909-593-3511 Fax 909-392-2711 Web.
www.ulv,edu Genealogy records of Church of the Brethren

Brethren Historical Archives 1451 Dundee Ave. Elgin,Ill.
60120 Tel 847-742-5100 Fax 847-742-6103 Web www.
brehtren.org/genbd

Bethany Theological Seminary 615 National Road Richmond,
Indiana 47374 Tel 1-800-287-8872
Web www.behhanyseminary.edu

McPherson College 1600 E. Euclid McPherson,Kansas 67460
Tel 316-241-0731 Web www.mcpherson.edu/library
Contains Church of the Brethren archives

Elizabethtown College High Library One Alpha Drive
Elizabethtown,Penna 17022 Tel 717-361-1451 Fax 717
361-1167 Web www.etown.edu/library

Brethren in Christ Archives Messiah College one College
Ave. Granthem,Penna 17027 Tel 717-691-6048 Fax 717-
691-6042 Web. www.messiah.edu/library National
archival repository for the Church of the Brethren

Juniata College 1815 Moore St. Huntingdon,Penna 16652
Tel 814-641-3000 Fax 814-641-3199 Web www.
juniata.edu

Ashland Theological Seminary 910 Center Street Ashland,
Ohio 44805 Tel 419-289-5168 Web www.ashland.edu
Trains clergy for the Church of the Brethren and has
Church of the Brethren historical materials.

First Church of the Brethren    2710 Kingston Rd.
    York,Pennsylvania    17402    Tel 717-755-0307

Bridgewater College Library    402 E. College St.
    Bridgewater,Virginia    22812    Tel 540-828-5411
    Fax 540-828-5482    Web www.bridgewater.edu/
    departments/library

# CHRISTIAN AND MISSIONARY ALLIANCE

This church originated in 1881 under the leadership of
Rev. A.B. Simpson,who left the Presbyterian Church to
carry on independent evangelistic work among the un-
churched.It was first divided into two societies;the
Christian Alliance for home missions,and the International
Missionary Alliance for work abroad. The two bodies were
merged in 1897 into the present Christian and Missionary
Today the church has about 200,000 members in the United.
States in about 1,500 congregations.

Nyack College/Alliance Theological Seminary  350 North
Highland Avenue  Nyack,New York  10960-3698.  Tel.
845-353-2020  Fax  845-348-3912  Web  www.nyack.edu/
ATS  Has materials back to the early history of C&MA.

Christian & Missionary Alliance Historical Library  P.O.
Box 35000  Tel 719-599-5999  Fax 719-593-8692  Web.
www.cmalliance.org  Materials dating back to the 1840s

Crown College  6425 County Road  St. Bonifacius,Minnesota
55375  Tel 952-446-4100  Fax 952-446-4149  Web
www.crown.edu/go/

Simpson University  2211 College View Drive  Redding,
California  96003  Tel 530-224-5600  Fax  530-226-4860
Web  www.simpson.edu

ToccoaFalls College  Seby Jones Library  Toccoa Falls,
Georgia  30598  Tel 706-886-6831  Fax 706-282-6005
Web  www.tfc.edu  Has materials on denominational
History as well as early history of the college.

# CHRISTIAN CHURCHES/DISCIPLES OF CHRIST

In this category are included the Independent Church of Christ and the Disciples of Christ. Each has more than 4,000 congregations and an excess of one million members in America.These groups were founded on the American frontier in the nineteenth century out of a deep concern for Christian unity. A key term in their historical development is the word "restoration" by which they mean a restoration to.New Testament pattern and pratice.

Barton College 400 Atlantic Christian University Dr. Wilson,North Carolina 27893. Tel 252-399-6500 Fax 252-399-6571 Web www. library.barton.edu Has Disciples of Christ archives for North Carolina.

Bethany College T.W. Phillips Library 300 Main St. Bethany,West Virginia 26042 Tel 304-829-7321 Fax 304-829-7333 Web www.bethany wv.edu/resources/library. Historical materials of Alexander Campbell and Disciples of Christ.

Boise Bible College 715 S. Capital Blvd. Boise, Idaho 83702 Tel 208-376-7731 Fax 208-376-7743 Web www.boisbible.edu Materials on restoration history

Butler University 4600 Sunset Indianapolis,Indiana 46208 Tel 317-940-9227 Fax 317-940-9711 Web www.butler.edu

Christian Theological Seminary 1000 W. 42 nd Indianapolis 46206 Tel 317-931-2367 Fax 317-931-2363 Web www.cts.edu

Culver Stockton College Library One College Hill Canton,Missouri 63435 Tel 573-288-6321 Fax 573-288-6615 Web www.culver.edu/library. This library has archival material

Disciples of Christ Historical Society  1101 19th
    Ave. South  Nashville,Tennessee  37682  Tel 615-
    327-4414  Fax  615-327-1445  Web  www.users.aol.
    com/dishistsoc  Has historical records from the
    Disciples of Christ,Independent Christian Churches,
    and Church of Christ

Drake University  2725 University Ave.  Des Moines,
    Iowa  50311  Tel 515-271-3993  Fax 515-271-3933
    Web  www.library.drake.edu

Emmanuel School of Religion Library  One Walker Dr.
    Johnson City,Tennessee  37601  Tel 423-926-1186
    Fax 423-926-6198  Web  www.esr.edu/library.htm
    Has both Christian Churches and Church of Christ
    records

Eureka College  301 E. College Ave  Eureka,Illinois
    61530  Tel 309-467-6380  Fax 309-467-6386  Web
    www.eureka.edu

Kentucky Christian University  Young Library  100
    Academic Place  Grayson,Kentucky 41143  Tel606-
    474-3240  Fax 606-474-3123 Web  www.kcu.edu/
    library  Operated by the Independent Christian
    Churches

Lexington Theological Seminary  631 S. Limestone
    Lexington,kentucky  40508  Tel 859-281-6042
    Fax 859-280-1229 Web www.library.lextheo.edu
    A Disciples of Christ school

Lincoln Christian College and Seminary  100 Campus
    View Dr. Lincoln,Illinois  62656  Tel217-732-
    7788  Fax 217-732-3785Web  www.kes.edu/library
    Maintains restoration archives

Manhattan Christian College  1415 Anderson Ave.
    Manhattan,Kansas  66502  Tel785-539-3571 Fax
    785-539-0832 Web  www.mccks.edu

Milligan College  Blowers Blvd.  Milligan Tenn.
    37682  Tel 423-461-8703  Fax  423-461-8964
    Web  www.milligan.edu/library

Ozark Christian College  1111 N. Main Street  Joplin,
   Missouri  64801  Tel417-626-1234 Fax 417-624-0090
   Web  www.occ.library.net  Independent Christian
   Churches archives

St. Louis Christian College Library  1369 Grandview
   Dr.  Florissant, Missouri  63033  Tel 314-837-6777
   Fax  314-837-8292  Web  www.slcc.4ministry.edu

Texas Christian University  2913 Lowden St.  Fort
   Worth, Texas  76129  Tel 817-257-7106 Fax 817-257-
   7112  Web  www.library.tcu.edu

Transylvania University  300 N. Broadway  Lexington,
   Kentucky  40508  Tel 859-233-8225  Fax 859-233-
   8779  Web  www.transy.edu/library

Northwest Christian University  828 E. 11th Avenue
   Eugene, Oregon  97401  Tel 541-684-7235  Fax 541-
   684-7307  Web  www.nwc.edu/library

# CHRISTIAN SCIENCE

The Church of Christ,Scientist,as it is properly called,had its roots in 1866 when Mary Baker Eddy recovered almost instantaneously from a severe injury while reading an account of Jesus' healing of a man sick of palsy in Matthew9:1-8 She wrote a book titled Science and Health With Key to the Scriptures. There are approximately 3,000 branches of the Mother Church which also maintain reading rooms that are open to the public.

Principia College  Marshall Brooks Library  Elsah, Illinois  62028  Tel 618-374-5235  Fax 618-374-5107 Cotains significant Christian Science historical records.

Boston Public Library  700 Boylston Street  Boston, Massachusetts  02117  Tel 617-536-5400 Fax 617-236-4306 Web  www.bpl.org

Christian Science Monitor Library  One Norway Street Boston,Massachusetts  02115

The First Church of Christ,Scientist  8221 Huntington Avenue  Boston,Massachusetts  02115  Tel

Union Theological Seminary  3041 Broadway  New York, New York  10022  Tel 212-280-1504  Fax 212-280-1314 Web  www.uts.edu Has early Christian Science collection

Foundation of Church of Christ,Science  1701 20th Street NW  Washington,D.C.  20009  Tel 202-797-9826  Fax  202-797-9813

# CHURCH OF CHRIST

This group represents a breakaway from the Disciples of Christ denomination and are made up primarily by the Church of Christ denomination with more than one million members

Faulkner University  6020 Atlanta Hwy  Montgomery, Ala. 36109  Tel 334-386-7207  Fax 334-386-7299  Web  www.faulkner.edu/library  Church of Christ

Pepperdine University Library  24255 Pacific Hwy Malibu, Calif. 90265  Tel 310-456-4252  Fax 310-456-4117  Web  www.pepperdine.edu

Oklahoma Christian College  Edmond, Okla  73013  Tel 800-877-5011

Harding Graduate School of Religion  1000 Cherry Memphis, Tenn 38117  Tel 901-761-1354  Web. www. hglib

Freed-Hardeman College  158 Main St.  Henderson, Tenn 38340  Tel 901-989-6067  Fax 907-989-6065 Web  www.fhu.edu/library

Johnson Bible College  7900 Johnson Drive  Knoxville, Tenn. 37998  Tel 865-251-2277  Fax 865-251-2278 Web  www.jbc.edu/library

Lipscomb University  One University Pk Dr.  Nashville, Tenn. 37203  Tel 615-956-1000  Web  www.lipscomb.edu/library

Abilene Christian University Library  Abilene, Texas 79699  Tel 325-674-3730  Fax  325-674-6180 Web  www.abcu.edu/library

Lubbock Christian University  5600 W. 19th Street Lubbock, Texas  79407  Tel 806-796-8800  Fax 806-796-8917  Web  www.lcu.edu/library.htm

# CHURCH OF GOD

At least 200 independent religious bodies in the United States bear the name of Church of God inone form or another with 3 having their headquarters in Cleveland,Tennessee,the largest of which has more than 500,000 members. Another significant group is headquartered in Anderson,Indiana with more than 200,000 members. Together there are more than one million members in all these groups

Anderson University Library  100 E. Fifth St Anderson,Indiana 46012  Tel 765-641-4290  Fax 765-
   641-3878  Web  www.anderson.edu  Has large Church
   of God archives

The University of Findlay  1000 N, Main St.  Findlay,
   Ohio  45840  Tel 419-434-4627  Fax 419-434-4196
   Web  www.findlay.edu/resources/library

Winebrenner Theological Seminary  950 N. Main Street
   Findlay,Ohio  45840  Tel 419-434-4200  Fax 419-
   434-4200  Fax 419-434-4267  Web  www.winebrenner.edu

Mid America Christian University  3500 SW 119th Street
   Oklahoma City,Okla.  73170  Tel 405-691-3800  Fax
   405-692-3172  Web  www.mabc.edu/library  Contains
   Church of God archives

Warner Pacific College  Otto Linn Library  2219 SE
   68th Ave  Portland,Oregon 97215  Tel 503-517-1034
   Web  www.warnerpacific.edu  Church of God archives

Lee University Church of God Theological Seminary  260
   11th St. NE  Cleveland,Tennessee 37311  Tel 423-614-
   8550  Fax 423-614-8555  Web  www.leeuniversity.edu/
   library

# EASTERN CHURCHES

Immigrants from traditional Eastern European countries came to America and established churches that used their native tongues in worship and continued deep ties with the old country. Today there are at least 15 national groups in America with names of their country of origin attached to their titles including Albanian, Bulgarian, Greek, Romanian, Russian, Serbian, Ukrainian, Carpatho-Russian,and Syrian. The largest of these is the Greek Archdiocese with nearly 2 million members.

Alaska Historical Library  State Office Bldg. Juneau, Alaska 99811  Tel 907-465-2910  Fax 907-465-2151 Web    www.eed.state.ak.us. Excellent collection of early Russian Orthodox settlememts.

St. Herman's Orthodox Seminary Library 414 Mission Road Kodiak,Alaska 99615  Tel 907-486-3524  Fax 907-486-5935. Has 4,000 books on Russian Orthodox in Alaska.

Serbian Eastern Orthodox Church  2311 M St. NW  Washington D.C. 20037 Web  http?oca.serbian - church.net.

St. Sava's School of Theology  32377 Milwaukee Avenue Libertyville,Illinois 60505  Tel 847-362-2440 Web www.midwestmetropolitinate.org. Trains priests for Serbian Orthodox Church and has records of churches.

Armenian Library and Museum  65 Main St. Watertown,Massachusetts 02172. Tel 617-929-2562  Fax 617-929-0175 Web www.almain.c 12,000 volumes of Armenian-American history

Hellenic College Library  50 Goddard Street  Brookline, Massachusetts 02146  Tel 617-850-2223  Fax 617-850-1470  Web  www.hchc.edu  Has 110,000 volumes with significant collection of Greek Orthodox history.

Albanian Orthodox Archdiocese  529 E. Broadway  Boston, Massachusetts 02127  Tel 617-268-1275  Fax 617-268-3184

Romanian Orthodox Episcopate  2535 Grey Tower Road Jackson,Michigan 49201  Tel 517-522-4800  Fax 517-522- 5907

St. Vladimir's Orthodox Theological Seminary 575
Scarsdale Road Yonkers,New York 10707 Tel 914
961-8313 Fax 914-961-4507 Web www.svots.edu
Over 100,000 volumes of Byzantine-American church
history.

St. Nersess Armenian Seminary Library 150 Stratton Road
New Rochelle,New York 10604 Tel 914-636-2004
Web www.stnersess.edu.

Antiochian Orthodox Archdiocese Box 5238 Englewood,
New York 10019 Tel 201-871-1355 Fax 201-871-7954
Web www.antiochian.org

Armenian Apostolic Church of America 138 E. 39th St.
New York,NY 10016 Tel 212-689-7168 Web www. arm
prelacy.org. Has 8,000 volumes on Armenian history

Bulgarian Eastern Orthodox Church 550-A W. 5oth St.
New York,NY 10019 Tel 212-246-4608 Fax 212-
489-3990

Greek Archdiocese of America 8-10 East 79th Street
New York,NY 10021 Tel 212-570-3500 Fax 212-570-
3569 Web www.goarch.org Records of Greek parishes back to early 19th century.

Holy Trinity Orthodox Seminary Box 31 Jordanville,
New York 13361 Tel 315-858-3116 Fax 315-858-
0945 Significant collection on Russian Orthodoxy.

Ukrainian Museum Archives 1202 Kenilworth Avenue
Cleveland,Ohio 44113 Tel 216-781-4329 Web www.
umacleveland.org 29,000 volumes of Ukrainian
church history back to the early 1900s.

Christ the Saviour Seminary 225 Chandler Street
Johnstown,Penna. 15902 Tel 814-539-8086 Web
www.seminary.acrod.org Contains records of the
Carpathian Russian Orthodox in America

St. Tikhons Orthodox Theological Seminary Box 130
South Canaan,Penna. 18499 Tel 570-937-4111
Fax 570-937-3100 Web. info@stot.edu

17

# EPISCOPAL

This is the American branch of the Church of England and is part of the worldwide Anglican Communion. The Episcopal Church came to America in 1578 when Sir Francis Drake established territory in Virginia. The church has parishes throughout America with a total membership of about 3 million. Several smaller groups also exist including the Reformed Episcopal Church, the Anglican Orthodox, and the Anglican Catholic having a total membership of less than 100,000.

Episcopal Diocese of Connecticut  1330 Asylum Ave.
Hartford, Conn. 01610  Tel 860-233-4481  Fax 860-523 1410  Web www.ctdiocese.org

Holy Trinity Church  606 Church St.  Wilmington, Delaware 19801  Tel 302-652-5627  Fax 302-652-8615  Web www.oldswedes.org

Episcopal Diocese of Massachusetts  138 Tremont Road  Boston, Mass 02111  Tel617-482-4826 Web www.dio mass.org  Has local diocesan histories

Episcopal Diocese of Missouri  1210 Locusr Street  St. Louis, Missouri  63101  Tel 314-231-1220  Fax 314-231-3373  diomissouri.org

General Theological Seminary  175 Ninth Ave  New York, NY 10011  Tel 212-243-5150  Fax 212-924-6304  Web www.library.gts.edu

Trinity Church Archives  74 Trinity Pl  New York, NY 10006  Tel 212-602-9652  Fax 212-602-9641  Web www.trinity wallstreet.org

Episcopal Diocese of Western North Carolina  Vance Ave.  Black Mountain, NC 28711  Reocords of 65 parishes in the diocese.

Reformed Episcopal Library  826 2 nd Ave. Blue Bell, Penna 19422  Tel 610-292-9852  Fax 610-292-9853  Web www.library.its.org/spetla/pts

Robert Carrother Library  15 Lippitt Rd  Kingston, R.I. 02881  Tel 401-874-2666  Fax 401-874-4608  Web www.uri.edu/library  Parish records from the diocese of Rhode Island

Voorhees College Voorhees Rd. Denmark, South Carolina
29042 Tel 803-793-0471 Web www.voorhees.edu

University of the South DuPont Library Sewanee,
Tenn. 37375 Tel 931-598-1364 Fax 931-598-1664
Web www.library.sewanee.edu

Archives of the Episcopal Church 600 Rathervue
Austin, Texas 78768 Tel 512-472-6816 Has records
from 1783 to present

Diocese of Olympia 1551 Tenth Ave. SE Seattle, Washington 98102 Tel 206-325-4200 Fax 206-325-4631
Records of the Episcopal Church in western Washington

Nashotah House Library 2777 Mission Rd. Nashotah,
Wisconsin 53058 Tel 262-646-6535 Fax 262-325-6564
Web www.nashotah.edu/library

## EVANGELICAL CONGREGATIONAL

This church body dates back to eastern Pennsylvania
in the 1920s when a group of clergy and congregations separated from the Evangelical Association.
Concentration of its 30,000 members in Pennsylvania,
Ohio, Illinois, and West Virginia. Headquarters and a
theological seminary are in Myerstown, Pennsylvania

Evangelical School of Theology  Rostad Library
    Myerstown, Pennsylvania 17067  Tel 717-866-5775
    Fax 717-866-4997  Web  www.evngelical.edu

# EVANGELICAL COVENANT

This church traces its roots back to Sweden and to the spiritual awakenings of the 19th century. It was brought to America by Swedish immigrants and numbers about 80,000 members in some 500 congregations. It maintains the North Park University and Theological Seminary in Chicago as well as the Swedish Covenant Hospital in that city.

North Park University Library  5114 N. Christiana Chicago,Illinois  60625  Tel 773-244-5580 Fax 773-244-4891  Web www.northparkedu/library Has archival materials and historical records

Swedish Historical Society  404 S. 3rd St. Rockford,Illinois 61104  Tel 815-963-5559

Swenson Swedish Immigration Research Center  3520 7 th Ave  Rock Island,Illinois  61201  Tel 309-794-7204  Fax  309-794-7443  Web  www.viking. augustana.edu/admin/swenson Has records of all Swedish denomination in America

American Swedish Institute  2600 Park Avenue Minneapolis,Minnesota  55407  Tel 612-871-4907 Fax 612-871-8682  Web  www.americanswedishinst.org

Fenton Historical Society  67 Washington St. Jamestown, New York  14701  Tel 716-664-6256 Fax 716-483-7524

New Sweden Historical Society  New Sweden,Maine 04762

# EVANGELICAL FREE CHURCH

This church has a Scandinavian background, being formed in 1950 from a merger of the Swedish Evangelical Free Church with the Norwegian-Danish Free Association. Its membership of 100,000 is now multi-ethnic with only about half being of Scandinavian background. It maintains a college and seminary near Chicago.

Trinity Evangelical Divinity School   2065 Half Day Road  Deerfield,Illinois 60015  Tel 847-317-4001 .Fax  847-317-4012  Web  www.tiu.edu/library. Has archives of the Evangelical Free Church

Swenson Swedish Immigration Research Center  3520 7th Ave.  Rock Island,Illinois 61201  Tel 309-794-7204  Fax 309-794-7443  Web  www.viking.augustana.edu/admin/swenson  Has records of all Scandinavian background churches

Evangelical Free Archives  1515 E 66th Street Minneapolis,Minnesota  55423  Tel 612-866-3343 National denominational archives

Sons of Norway Library  1455 W. Lake  Minneapolis, Minnesota  55608  Tel 612-827-3611  Fax 612-945-8551  Web.  www.sonsofnorway.com

The American Swedish Institute  2600 Park Avenue Minneapolis,Minnesota  55407  Tel 612-821-4907 Fax  612-821-8682

Norwegian American Historical Association  St.Olaf College  Northfield, Minnesota  55057  Tel 507-646-3221  Fax 507-646-3734  Web  www.naha.stolaf.edu

# SOCIETY OF FRIENDS (QUAKERS)

With a membership of only 125,000 in the U.S.
the Society of Friends has had a deep and last-
ing effect on western society.They foubd a home
in William Penn's colony where they established
a model of peaceful coexistence. They are trad-
itionally pacifist and work in copperation with
other groups.There are sevarl other related groups
including the Friends General Conference and the
Friends United Meeting.

Whittier College Wardmann Library Whittier,
    California 90608 Tel 562-907-4220 Fax 562-
    693-6117 Web www.whittier.edu/fairchild/
    home

Earlham College 801 National Road Richmond,
    Indiana47374 Tel 765-983-1360 Fax 765-
    983-1287 Web www.earlham.edu/library
    Collection of Quaker materials of Indiana

William Penn University Wilcox Library Okaloosa
    Iowa 52577 Tel 641-673-1096 Fax 641-673-
    1098 Web www.williampenn.edu/library

Friends University 2100 W. University Avenue
    Wichita,Kansas 67213 Tel 316-261-5842 Fax
    316-295-5880 Web www.friends.edu/academics/
    library

Malone College 2600 Cleveland Ave. Canton,Ohio
    44709 Tel 330-471-8317 Fax 330-454-6977
    Web www.malone.edu/academics/library

Salem Public Library 821 E. State St. Salem,
    Ohio 44460 Tel 330-332-0042 Fax 330-332-
    4488 Web www.salemohio.com/library

Wilmington College Watson Library 1870 Quaker
    Way Wimington,Ohio 45177 Tel 937-382-6661
    Fax 937-383-8571 Web www.watsonlibrary.org

George Fox University 416 N. Meridian Newburg, Oregon 97132 Tel 503-554-2410 Fax 503-554-2419 Web www.library.georgefox.edu

Haverford College 370 Lancaster Avenue Haverford, Pennsylvania 19041 Tel 610-896-1175 Fax 610-896-1102 Web www.haverford.edu/library Collection includes 17th century Quaker literature

Friends Free Library of Germantown 5418 Germantown Avenue Philadelphia,Penna 19144 Tel 215-951-2355 Fax 215-951-2697 Web www.germantownfriends.org

Historical Society of Pennsylvania 1300 Locust St. Philadelphia,Penna 19107 Tel 215-732-6200 Fax 215-732-2680 Web www.hsp.org Has extensive early Quaker records

Philadelphia Yearly Meeting of the Religious Society of Friends 1515 Cherry Street Philadelphia,Penna 19102 Tel 215-241-7220 Fax 215-567-2096 Web www.pym.org/library

Friends Historical Society Swarthmore College 500 College Drive Swarthmore,Pennsylvania 19081 Tel 610-328-8496 Fax 610-690-5728 Web www.swarthmore.edu/library

Western Yearly Meeting of Friends 203 East Street Plainfield,Indiana 46168 Tel 317-839-2789 Web www.westernym.net

# ISLAMIC

Prior to the 1960s the Muslim population in the U.S.
was about one million and there were probably no
more than 100 functioning mosques. With the flow of
immigrants from Muslim countries as Iraq, Iran, Pak-
istan, and Egypt there are more than 500 mosques ser-
ving more than five million Muslim-Americans. They
tend to gravitate toward large cities with 20%
living in California, 16% in New York, and 8% in
Indiana.

Ahmadiyya Movement of Islam Library  2141 Leroy Pl
    NW  Washington, D.C. 20008  Tel 202-232-3737  Fax
    202-232-8181  Web  www.alislam.org

America's Islamic Heritage Museum  2315 Martin Luther
    King Ave SE  Washington, D.C. 20008  Tel 202-678-
    6906  Web  www.muslimsinamerica.org

American Islamic College  840 W. Irving Park Rd.
    Chicago, Illinois  Tel 773-281-4700

Islamic Society of North America  P.O. Box 38
    Plainfield, Indiana  46168

Islamic Association of North America  3588 Plymouth
    Road  Ann Arbor, Michigan  48105  Web  www.iana
    @iananet.org

## JEHOVAH'S WITNESS

This group had its origins in a Bible study movement of the 1870's under Restoration leader,Charles
Taze Russell. In 880 the Watchtower Tract Society
formed.Among their teachings is a belief that the
end of the world is imminent. There are about
565,000 members in 7,500 congregations in the
United States.

International Headquarters  25 Columbia Heights
    Brooklyn,New York  11201

Watchtower Bible School of Gilead Library 25
    Columbia Heights  Brookly,New York  11201
    Tel 718-560-5000  Web  www.watchtower.org

## JEWISH

Jews arrived early with American colonists,some living in Peter Stuyvasant's New Amsterdam in the 1650s. As European immigration increased along with persecution of Jews in Europe,the number of Jews migrating to America likewise increased. Germany,France. Spain, Czechoslovakia, Poland, and Hungary were the major nations from which they came. Today there are more than 5 million Jews in America in 5,000 synagogues. American Judaism is divided among 3 groups - Orthodox, Conservative, and Reform. They have done much to preserve their historical records

Western Jewish Historical Center 2911 Russell St. Berkeley,California 94705 Tel 510-331-5908 Fax 510-849-3673

Brandeis Bardin Institute 1101 Pepperdine Lane Brandeis, California 93064 Tel 805-582-4450 Fax 805-526-1398 Web www.thebbi.org

Hebrew Union College 3077 University Ave. Los Angeles, California 90007 Tel 213-765-2127 Fax 213-749-1937 Web www.huc.edu/libraries

Jewish Community Library 6505 Wilshire Blvd. Los Angeles, California 90048 Tel 323-761-8644 Fax 323-861-8647 www.jella.org.

Institute of Judaism Library 15600 Mulholland Drive Los Angeles,California 90077 Tel 310-476-9777 Fax 310-476-5423

Bureau of Jewish Education 601 14th Ave San Francisco, California 94118 Tel 415-567-3327 Fax 415-567-6542 Web www.bjesf.org.

Colorado Library for Jewish Education 300 S. Dahlia St. Denver,Colorado 80246 Tel 303-321-3191 Fax 303-321-5346 Web www.caje-co.org

Rocky Mountain Jewish Historical Society 2040 E. Evans Denver,Colorado 80208 Tel 303-871-3020 Fax 303-871-3037

George Washington University Gelman Library 2130 H St NW Washington,DC 20057 Tel 202-994-6455 Fax 202-994-6464 Web www.gwu.edu/gelman

Central Agency for Jewish Educational Resource Center 4200 Biscayne Bld. Miami, Florida 33137 Tel 305-576-4080 Fax 305-576-0307 Web www.caje-miami.org Records of Judaism in south Florida.

Spertus Institute of Jewish Studies  618 S. Michigan
Ave.  Chicago,Illinois 60605  Tel 312-322-1712.
Fax 312-922-04555  Web www.spertus.edu

Hebrew Theological College  7135 N. Carpenter Rd.
Skokie,Illinois 60077  Tel 847-982-2500  Fax 847-
-674-6381  Web www.htcnet.edu

Jewish Museum of Maryland Library  15 Loyd St.  Balt-
imore.Maryland 21202  Tel410-732-6400  Fax 410-732-
6451 Web www.jhsm.org  Records of Judaism in the
Maryland area.

National Yiddish Book Center Library  1021 W Street
Wshington,DC 20001  Tel 413-256-4900  Fax 413-256-
6541  Web www.yiddishbookcenter.org  Has a stock
of over one million books.

American Jewish Historical Society  2 Thornton Road
Waltham,Massachusetts  02453  Tel 781-736-4724
Fax 781-899-9208  Web www.ajhs.org

Brandeis University Library  415 South St.  Waltham,
Massachusetts 02454  Tel 781-736-7777  Fax 781-
736-4719 Web www.library.brandeis.edu.

Jewish Community Center of Metropolitan Detroit  6600
W. Maple  West Bloomfield,Michigan 48322  Tel 248-
661-7639  Fax 248-6661-3680  Maintains 11,000
volumes of books on American Jewish history.

Kripke Jewsish Federation Library  333 S. 132nd St.
Omaha,Nebraska  68154  Tel 402-334-6461  Fax 402-
334-6464  Web Jewishomaha.org

American Jewish Committee  Blaustein Library  165 E.
56th St. New York,NY 10022  Tel 212-751-4000  Fax212
891-1470

American Jewish Congress  15 E. 84th St.  New York,NY
10028  Tel 212-879-4500  Fax 212-758-1633

Jewish Theological Seminary Library  3080 Broadway
New York,NY 10028  Tel 212-678-8075  Fax 212-678-
8891  Web www.jtsa.edu/library

Yeshiva University Library  500 W. 185th Street  New
York,NY 10033  Tel 212-960-5363  Fax 212-960-0066

Hebrew Union College Klau Library 3101 Clifton
Avenue Cincinnati,Ohio 45220 Tel 513-487-3287.
Fax 513-221-0519 Web www.huc.edu

Center for Judaic Studies 420 Walnut St. Philadelphia,
Penna. 19106 Tel 215-238-1290 Web www.library.
upenn.edu/cjs

Philadelphia Jewish Archives Center 18 S. 7th Street
Philadelphia,Penna 19106 Tel,215-925-8090 Fax
215-925-4413 Web www.library.upenn.edu/cjs

Philadelphia Jewish Archives 18 S. 7th Street
Philadelphia,Penna 19106-1423 Tel 215-925-8090
Fax 215-925-4413 Web www.libertynet,org/pjac

Reconstructionist Rabbinical College 1299 Church Rd.
Wyncote,Penna 19095 Tel 215-576-0800 Fax 215-
576-6143 Web www.wrrr.edu

Jewish Federation Libraries 809 Percy Warren Blvd.
Nashville, Tenn. 37205 Tel 615-356-1880 Fax
615-356-1850 Web. www.jewishnashville.org

Beth Abahah Museum and Archives 1109 E. Franklin
Richmond,Virginia 23220 Tel 804-353-2668 Web
www.bethabahah.org

LATTER DAY SAINTS (MORMONS)

Better known as the Mormons this movement began
with Joseph Smith in New York who reported having a series of heavenly revelations. The major
portion of them gradually settled in Utah where
they established Salt Lake City. Today there are
more than fivr million members in five different
groups, the main one being the Church of Jesus
Christ of Latter Day Saints.

Staff Family History Center  1530 W. Camino Real
   Boca Raton, Florida  33486  Tel 561-395-6644
   Fax 561-395-8957

Brigham Young University  55-220 Kilanui Street
   Laie, Hawaii  96762  Tel 808-675-3876  Fax 808-
   675-3877  Web  www.library.byoh.edu

Brigham Young University of Idaho  525 S. Center
   St.  Rexburg, Idaho  83460  Tel208-496-9524
   Fax 208-496-9503  Web www.lib.byui.edu

Graceland University  One University Place
   Lamoni, Iowa  50140  Tel 641-784-5196  Fax 641-
   784-5301  Web  www.graceland.edu/library/index

Reorganized Church of Latter Day Saints  201 North
   River  Independence, Missouri  Web  www.rids.org

Brigham City Library  26 E. Forest  Brigham City.
   Utah  84302  Tel 435-723-5850  Fax 435-723-2813
   Web  www.bcpl.lib.ut.us

Utah State University Library  800 W. University
   Parkway  Orem, Utah  84058  Tel 801-863-8751
   Fax 801-863-7065  Web  www.uvsc.ed/library

Brigham Young University Library  2720 HBLL  Provo,
   Utah  84602  Tel 801-422-3593  Fax 801-422-0404
   Web  www.byu.edu/library

Church of Jesus Christ of Latter Day Saints  50
    East North Temple. Salt Lake City,Utah 84150
    Tel  801-240-2202  Fax 801-240-1845  Web  www.
    lds.org/churchhistory.  The main source of
    Mormon genealogical history

Family History Center  35 North West Temple Street.
    Salt Lake City,Utah  84150  Tel 801-240-2584
    Fax 801-240-3718  Web .www.familysearch.org

Salt Lake City Public Library  209 E. 500 South
    Salt Lake City,Utah  84111  Tel 801-524-8200
    Fax 801-364-4661  Web  www.slepl.lib.ut.us

Weber State University  2901 University Circle
    Ogden,Utah  84408  Tel 801-626-6402  Fax 801-
    626-7045  Web  www.library.weber.edu

# LUTHERAN

Lutherans came to America primarily from Germany and the Scandinavian countries. Originally the American church was divided into synods based on national origin. Today there are three major bodies:the Evangelical Lutheran Church in America, the Lutheran Church-Missouri Synod,and the Wisconsin Evangelical Lutheran Synod. There are about 8 million Lutherans in America making them the third largest Protestant group.

Archives of the ELCA - Region 1  Mortvedt Library  Pacific Lutheran University  Tacoma,Washington  98447  Tel 253-535-7586  Web www.plu.edu-archives

Archives of the ELCA - Region 2  Pacific Lutheran Theological Seminary.2770 Marin Ave.  Berkeley, California  Tel 510-524-5264

Archives of the ELCA - Region 3  2481 Como Avenue  St. Paul,Minnesota  55108  Tel.651-641-3205

Archives of the ELCA - Region 4 Bethany Lutheran College  Wallerstedt Library  Lindsborg,Kansas  67456  Tel 785-227-3311

Archives of the ELCA - Region 5  Wartburg Theological Seminary  Dubuque,Iowa  52003  Tel.563-589-0320

Archives of the ELCA - Region 6  Trinity Lutheran Seminary 2199 East Main St.  Columbus,Ohio 43209  Tel 614-235-4136  Web www.tlsohio.edu/elca-region-6-archives

Archives of the ELCA - Region 7  Lutheran Theological Seminary  7301 Germantown Avenue  Philadelphia,Penna 19119  Tel 215-248-6329  Web www.ltsp.edu/krauth/index.html

Archives of the ELCA - Region 8  Thiel College  75 College Ave.  Greenville,Penna 16125  Tel 724-589-2124  Web www.thiel.edu

Archives of the ELCA - Region 9  Lutheran Theological Southern Seminary  4201 Main St.  Columbia,SC 29203  Tel 803-461-3234  Web www.crumleyarchives.org

Bishop Wilma Kucharek   P.O. Box 1003   Torrington,
Connecticut   06790   Tel 860-482-6100.  Records
of Slovak Lutherans

Lutheran Church-Missouri Synod Central Library
1333 S. Kirkwood Road   St. Louis,Missouri 63105
Tel 314-965-9000 Fax  314-822-8307  Records of
congregations of the Lutheran Church-Missouri
Synod

Concordia Historical Institute   804 Seminary Place
St. Louis,Missouri 63105  Tel 314-505-7900 Fax
314-505-7901 Web  www.lutheranhistory.org

Wisconsin Evangelical Lutheran Synod   2929 North
Mayfair  Milwaukee,Wisconsin   53227   Tel 414-
256-3888

Luther College Library   700 College Dr.  Decorah,
Iowa 52101   Tel 563-387-1166   Web  www.luther.
edu/research Records of Norwegian Lutherans

Vesterheim Norwegian-American Museum  523 W. Water
St. Decorah,Iowa 52101  Tel 563-382-9681  Fax
563-382-8828.  Web   www.vesterheim.org

Grand View University Library   1350 Morton Drive
Des Moines,Iowa  50316   Tel 515-263-2877  Web
www.gvc.edu   Records of Danish Lutherans

Finnish American Heritage Center  435 Quincy St.
Hancock,Michigan  49930   Tel 906-487-7347
Web  www.finlandia.edu/fahs  Finnish Lutheran
archives

Finlandia University  601 Quincy St.  Hancock,Mich.
49930  Tel 906-487-7252  Web  www.finlandia.edu/
maki-library

Danish Immigrant Museum  2212 Washington Street
Elk Horn,Iowa  51531  Tel 712-764-7001

Swenson Swedish Immigration Research Center  3520
7th Ave. Rock Island,Illinois 61201   Tel 309-
794-7204  Web  www.augustana.edu/swenson

American Swedish Institute and Archives  2600
    Park Ave. Minneapolis,Minnesota  55407  Tel
    612-871-3354  Fax 612-641-3354  Web  www.
    americanswedishinstitute.org

Gustavus Adolphus College  Bernadotte Library
    800 W. College Ave.  St. Peter,Minn. 56082
    Tel 507-933-7556  Fax  507-933-7558  Web
    www.gustavus.edu/library  Records of Swedish
    Lutheran churches and families

Norwegian-American Historical Association  St.
    Olaf College  Rovaag Library  1510 St. Olaf
    Avenue  Northfield,Minnesota 55057  Tel 507-
    786-3221  Fax  507-786-3734  Web  www.naha.
    stolaf.edu

Church of the Lutheran Brethren  1020 W. Alcott
    Fergus Falls,Minnesota  56538  Tel 218-739-
    3336  Fax  218-739-5514

Evangelical Lutheran Synod  6 Browns Court
    Mankato,Minnesota  56001  Primarily Norwegian
    Lutherans

Apostolic Lutheran Church  Web  www.apostolic-
    lutheran.org  Records of Finnish Lutherans
    dating back more than a century

# MENNONITE

Mennonites derive their name from Menno Simons, a former Roman Catholic priest who disagreed with Swiss reformer Ulrich Zwingli and started a congregation in Zurich, Switzerland in 1525. They came to America settling primarily in Pennsylvania, Ohio, Virginia, Indiana, and Kansas where they established colleges. There are 16 Mennonite bodies in America with a membership of about 250,000. The largest of these is the Mennonite Church with about 100,000 members.

Fresno Pacific University Hiebert Library 1717 So. Chestnut Ave Fresno, California 93702 Tel 559-453-2090 Fax 559-453-2007 Web www.fresno.edu/dept/library. Records and center for Mennonite Brethren studies.

Associated Mennonite Biblical Seminary Library 3003 Benham Elkhart, Inidiana 46517 Tel 219-296-6253 Fax 219-295-0092 Web www.ambs.edu/library

Mennonite History Library So. Main Street Goshen, Indiana 46526 Tel 219-535-7418 Fax 219-535-7438 Web www.goshen.edu

Kalona Public Library 511 C Ave Kalona, Iowa 52247 Tel 319-656-3501 Fax 319-656-3503 Web www.kctc.net/kalopublic Records of Amish history

Mennonite Library and Archives 300 E. 27th St. North Newton, Kansas 67117 Tel 316-284-5304 Fax 316-284-5286 Web www.bethelks.edu

Tabor College Library 400 S. Jefferson St. Hillsboro, Kansas 67063 Tel 316-947-3121 Fax 316-947-2607 Web www.tabor.edu Mennonite Brethren archives.

Western District of the General Conference Mennonites P.O. Box 306 North Newton, Kansas 67117 Tel 316-283-6300 Fax 316-283-0620 Web www.mennowbe.org

Bluffton College Library 280 W. College Ave Bluffton, Ohio 45817 Tel 419-358-3271 Fax 419-358-3384 Web www.bluffton.edu/library

Burton Public Library  14588 W. Park  Burton,Ohio
    44021  Tel 440-834-4466  Fax  440-834-0128  Web
    www.burton.lib.oh.us   Amish archives

Holmes County District Public Library  3102 Glen Dr.
    Millersburg,Ohio  44654  Tel 330-674-5972  Fax
    330-674-1938  Web  www.holmes.lib.oh.us  Has
    Amish and Mennonite historical documents

Mennonite Historians of Eastern Pennsylvania  565
    Yoder Rd.  Harleysville,Penna.  19438  Web
    www.mhep.org

Lancaster Mennonite Historical Society  535 W. James
    St.  Lancaster,Penna.  17603  Tel 717-290-8707
    Fax 717-393-4254  Web  www.lts.org

Zion Memorial Church and Public Library  149 Cherry
    Lane   Soudertown,Penna.  Tel 215-723-3592

Eastern Mennonite University Library  1200 Park Road
    Harrisonburg,Virginia  22802  Tel 540-432-4175
    Fax 540-432-4977  Web  www.emu.edu/library

## MORAVIAN

The Moravian Church has roots dating back to the 9th century, but became organized with the martyrdom of Jan Hus in 1415. Moravians came to America in the 18th century establishing the towns of Bethlehem, Nazareth, and Lititz in Pennsylvania and Salem in North Carolina. The church has a membership of about 60,000 and there is also a smaller group centered in Texas known as the Czech-Moravian Brethren which has about 6,000 members.

Moravian Archives - Southern Province 457 S. Church Street Winston-Salem, North Carolina Tel 336-722-1742 Fax 336-725-4514 Web www.moravianarchives.org. Historical records of the southern province

Moravian Music Foundation 457 S. Church Street Winston-Salem, North Carolina 27101 Tel 336-725-0651 Fax 336-725-4514

Salem College 626 S. Church Street Winston-Salem, North Carolina 27108 Tel 336-721-2649 Fax 336-917-5339 Web www.salem.edu

Moravian Archives 41 W. Locust Street Bethlehem, Pennsylvania 18018 Tel 610-866-3255 Fax 610-866-9210

Moravian College and Theological Seminary 1200 Main Bethlehem, Pennsylvania 18018 Tel 610-861-1541 Fax 610-861-1544 Web www.moravian.edu/public/reeves/index

Moravian Historical Society 214 E. Center Street Nazareth, Pennsylvania 18064 Tel 215-759-0292 Records dating back to 1740

# NAZARENE

This group,with Methodist background,adheres to the original Wesleyan theology. It was formed from the merger of two previous Nazarene bodies, one in New York and the other in New England. There are about one helf million members in the United States in about 5,000 congregations.

Point Loma Nazarene University 3900 Lomaland Dr. San Diego,California 92106 Web www.ptloma.edu

Northwest Nazarene University 623 University Blvd. Nampa,Idaho 83686 Tel 208-467-8096 Fax 208-467-8611 Web www.nmu.edu/library

Olivet Nazarene University One University Avenue Bourbonnnais,Illinois 60914 Tel 815-939-5204 Fax 815-939-5354 Web www.library.olivet.edu

Mid-Atlantic Nazarene University 2030 College Way Olathe,Kansas 66062 Tel 913-971-3485 Fax 913-971-3285 Web www.mnu.edu/mabee

Eastern Nazarene College 23 E. Elm Street Quincy, Massachusetts 02170 Tel 617-745-3850 Fax 617-745-3913 Web www.library.enc.edu

Nazarene Theological Seminary 1700 E. Myer Blvd. Kansas City,Missouri 64131 Tel 816-268-3471 Fax 816-822-9025 Web www.nts.edu

Nazarene Archives 6401 The Paseo Kansas City, Missouri 64131 Tel 816-333-7000 Has church national archives dating back to 1916

Southern Nazarene University 4115 N. College
Bethany, Oklahoma 73008 Tel 405-491-6351
Fax 405-491-6355 Web www.ruth.snu.edu

Trevecca Nazarene 73 Lester Avenue Nashville,
Tennessee 37210 Tel 615-248-1714 Fax 615-
248-1570 Web www.maclib.trevecca.edu

Mount Vernon Nazarene University Thorne Library
Learning Resources Center 800 Martinsburg
Road Mount Vernon, Ohio 43050 Tel 740-397-
9000 Fax 740-397-8847 Web www.mvnc.edu

# PENTECOSTAL

Pentecostal is an inclusive term applied to a large
number of revivalistic American sects,assemblies,
and churches many of whom came from a Methodist or
Baptist background. Unlike many churches with roots
in Europe Pentecostal groups were born in America.
The largest of these groups is the Assemblies of
God with 1.5 million members in 10,000 congregations. There are at least twelve additional Pentecostal denominations including the Pentecostal
Holiness Church and the Pentecostal Church of God.

Assemblies of God Archives   1441 Boonville Avenue
    Springfield,Missouri   65802

Assemblies of God Theological Seminary   1455 Glen
    Springfield,Missouri   65802   Tel 412-268-1000
    Fax 412-268-1004   Web www.agts.edu

Central Bible College   300 N. Grant   Springfield,
    Missouri   Web   www.cbcag.du/library

Beulah Heights University   Barth Memorial Library
    892 Berne St. SE   Atlanta,Georgia 30316   Tel
    404-627-2631   Fax 404-627-0702   Web   www.
    beulah.org

Southwestern Christian University   7210   NW 39th
    Expressway   Bethany,Oklahoma   73008   Tel 405-
    789-7661   Fax 405-495-0078   Web   www.sculibrary.
    blogspot.com

Oral Roberts University   7777 S. Lewis   Tulsa,
    Oklahaoma   74105   Tel 918-495-6723   Fax 918-495-
    6893   Web   www.oru.edu/library

Northwest University   5520 108th Ave NE   Kirkland,
    Washington 98033   Tel 425-889-5266   Fax 425-889-
    7801   Web   www.librarynorthwestu.edu. Contains
    Pentecostal records of the Pacific Northwest.

# POLISH NATIONAL CATHOLIC

After long years of dissatisfaction with Roman Catholic administration and policies and with a desire for religious freedom this body was organized in 1897. It is catholic in theology and liturgy but does not recognize the primacy of the Papacy. There are about 280,000 members in 160 parishes in the United States and Canada.

Polish National Catholic Church Headquarters 1006 Pittston Avenue. Scranton, Pennsylvania 18505 Tel 570-346-9131 Has records of parishes in the United States and Canada

Savonarola Theological Seminary 1031 Cedar St. Scranton, Pennsylvania 18505 Tel 570-346-9131

PRESBYTERIAN

Presbyterian history dates back to John Calvin,a
Frenchman who established a theocracy in Geneva,
Switzerland. Presbyterianism found it greatest
success in Scotland from whence it came to the
United States. Presbyterians quickly spread in
America making it a truly national denomination.
The United Presbytreian Church is the largest
group with about 2.5 million members,but there
are eight other groups including the Associate
Reformed,the Orthodox,and the Cumberland churches

Columbia Theological Seminary  701 Columbia Drive
    Decatur,Georgia  30031  Tel 404-687-4549 .Fax
    404-687-4687  Web  www.ctsnet.edu/library

Hanover College  121 Scenic Drive. Hanover,Indiana
    47243  Tel 812-866-7165  Fax 812-866-7172 Web
    www.hanover.edu/library.Indiana church archives

Louisville Presbyterian Theological Seminary 1044
    Alta Vista Road  Louisville,Kentucky 40205  Tel
    502-895-3411  Fax 502-895-1096  Web  www.lpts.
    edu/library

Covenant Theological Seminary  12330 Conway Road
    St. Louis,Missouri 63141  Tel 314-434-4044  Fax
    314-434-4819  Web  www.covenantseminary.edu
    Has Presbyterian Church in America archives

Belhaven College  Hood Library  Jackson,Mississippi
    39202  Tel 601-969-7400 Web  www.blehaven.edu/
    hood

Princeton University  One Washington Road  Princeton,
    New Jersey 08544  Tel 609-497-7940  Fax  609-497-
    1826  Web  www.libweb.princeton.edu

Davidson College  202 D Road  Davidson,North Carolina
    28036  Tel 704-894-2331  Fax 704-894-2625  Web
    www.davidson.edu

Presbyterian Historical Society   318 Georgia Terr.
Montreat,North Carolina 28757  Web  www.history.
pcusa.org

Presbyterian Historical Society   425 Lombard Street
Phuladelphia,Penna 19147  Tel 215-627-1852  Fax
215-627-0509  Web www.history.pcusa.org  Has
national archives dating from 1706

Geneva College   3200 College Ave   Beaver Falls,
Penna. 15010  Tel 724-8426-764  Fax 724-8426-
6687  Web www.geneva.edu  Has documents from
Reformed Presbyterian history

Presbyterian Theological Seminary   616 N. Highland
Ave.  Pittsburgh,Penna 15206  Tel 412-924-1354
Fax  412-362-2329  Web www.barbourlibrary.org

Reformed Presbyterian Theological Seminary   7418
Penn Ave.  Pittsburgh,Penna  15208  Tel 412-731-
8690  Fax  412-731-4834

Presbyterian College   211 East Maple Street   Clinton,
South Carolina  29325  Tel 864-833-8299  Fax
864-833-8315  Web www.presbyterian.edu/library
Documents in denominational history

Erskine College   College Drive Due West,South Car-
olina 29629  Tel 864-379-8898  Fax  864-379-2900
Web www.erskine.edu/library  Has records of the
Associate Reformed Presbyterian Churches

Associate Reformed Presbyterian Archives  Cleveland
Street  Greenville,South Carolina  29601  Tel
864-232-8297  Fax  864-271-3729  Web www.arp
church.org

King College  1350 King College Road  Bristol,
Tennessee  37620  Tel 423-652-4716  Fax 423-
652-4871  Web  www.king.edu/library  Has a
southern Presbyterian historical collection

Union Theological Seminary of Virginia  3401 Brook
Road  Richmond,Virginia  23227  Tel 804-278-4310
Fax 804-278-4375  Web  www.library.union.psce.
edu  Records of the Synod of Virginia

Whitworth University  300 West Hawthorne Road
Spokane,Washington 99251  Tel 509-777-3260
Fax 509-777-3221  Web  www.whitworth.edu Has
documents of Protestant church work in the
Pacific Northwest

Reformed Theological Seminary  5422 Clinton Ave.
Jackson,Mississippi 39209  Tel 601-923-1623
Fax  601-923-1621  Web  www.rts.edu/library
Has records of southern Presbyterian history

Bethel University  325 Cherry Ave  McKenzie,Tenn-
essee 38201  Tel 731-352-4083  Fax 731-352-4010
Web  www.betheluniversity.edu/library  Has a
large collection of Cumberland Presbyterian
church histories

Memphis Theological Seminary  168 E. Parkway South
Memphis,Tennessee 38018  Tel 901-334-5812  Fax
901-452-4051  Web  www.mtscampus.edu/library
Cumberland Presbyterian archives.

# REFORMED

The Reformed churches date back to 16th century
Europe and were prominent in Holland,England,and
Scotland. There are six major groups in America
with the largest being the Reformed Church in
America with about 400,000 members and the Christian
Reformed Church of about 300,000 both of which are
primarliy of Dutch background.

Northwester College  101 7th St SW  Orange City,Iowa
51041  Tel713-707-7234  Fax 712-707-7247
Web  www.nwciowa.edu

Central College Library 812 University Street  Pella,
Iowa 50219  Tel641-628-5193  Fax 641-628-5327
Web  www.central.edu/library

Calvin College  3207 Burton St.  Grand Rapids,Michigan
49546  Tel 616-526-8573 Fax 616-526-6470  Web www.
calvin.edu/library  National archives of the Christian
Reformed Church

Hope College  53 Graves Pl.  Holland,Michigan  49422
Tel 616-392-8555  Fax616-392-8554  Web www.hope.edu
/lib

Joint Archives of Holland  Hope College Library
Tel 616-395-7798 Web www.hope.edu/jointarchives
Oral histories of the Reformed Church in America

First Christian Reformed Church  15 S. Church  Zeeland,
Michigan  49464  Tel 616-772-2866
Church history and acts of Synod from 1815-present

Eden Webster Library  475 n. Lockwood  St. Louis,Missouri
63119  Tel314-968-6950  Fax 314-968-7113
Web  www.library.webster.edu

New Brunswick Theological Seminary  21 Seminary Place
New Brunswick,New Jersey  08901  Tel 732-247-5243
Web www.nbts.edu  Archives of The Reformed Church
in America

Dordt College Library 498 4th Avenue N.E.
Sioux Center,Iowa 51250 Tel 712-722-6040
Fax 712-722-1198 Web www.dordt.edu/services/
library Has a signficant collection of Dutch
and Reformed Church history

Chr istian Reformed Church Library P.O. Box 3
New Holland,South Dakota 57365 Tel 605-243-2346

# ROMAN CATHOLIC

While Catholics came to American shores with
such explorers as Columbus and Coronado the
first permanent parish in America was at St.
Augustine, Florida in 1565. Later a colony was
established in Maryland but growth was slow
until the early 19th century when a steady
flow of immigrants from souther and eastern
Europe helped the numbers grow to about 6
million by 1900.

Baltimore became the first American diocese
in 1789 and New York and Philadelphia were
to follow shortly thereafter. During the 20th
century the Catholic Church grew rapidly so
that at the end of the century there were
about 50 million catholic in the United States
or about 23% of the American population.

These 50 million faithful are served by more
than 50,000 priests in 32 archidoceses and
137 dioceses.

Catholic Diocese of Fairbanks  1316 Pege Rd
Fairbanks, Alaska 99709. Tel. 907-374-9500
Fax  907-374-9580 Web  www.cbna.org

Academy of American Franciscan History Studies
1712 Euclid Ave.  Berkeley, Calif. 94709.
Tel. 510-548-1755. Fax 510-548-9466  Web
www.aath.org

Roman Catholic Diocese of Fresno  1550 N Fresno
St.  Fresno, Calif. 93703  Tel 559-488-7400
Fax  559-488-7464

Archdiocese of San Francisco  320 Middlefield Rd.
Tel 650-328-6512

Regis University  Dayton Memorial Library  3333
Regis Blvd.  Denver, Colorado  Tel 303-458-4030
Fax 303-964-5497  Web  www.regis.edu Valuable
reference of Jesuit work in the southwest

St. Thomas Seminary  467 Bloomfield Ave.  Bloomfield
Conn. 06002  Tel  860-242-5573  Fax 860-242-4886
Web  www.sts.pages

Catholic University of America   620 Michigan Ave NE
   Wash. DC 20017   Tel. 202-319-5055   FAX 202-319-4735
   Web www.libraries.cua.edu

Georgetown University  3700 O St. NW  Wash. DC 20057
   Tel 202-687-7425  Fax 202-687-7501  Web  www.
   library.georgetown.edu

DePaul University Library  2350 N. Kenmore  Chicago,Ill.
   60201  Tel 773-325-3725  Fax 773-325-7870 Web.
   www.lib.depaul.edu  Valuable history of Vincentians

Loyola University Library  25 E. Pearson St.  Chicago,
   Ill  60611  Tel 773-508-2632 Wash. www.libraries.luc,edu
   Extensive Jesuit materials

St. Mary of the Woods College Library  St. Mary of the
   Woods,Indiana 47876  Tel 812-535-5221  Fax 812-535-5127
   Web www.smc.edu

St. Meinrad School of Theology  One Hill Drive  St.
   Meinrad,Indiana 47577  Tel 812-357-6401  Fax 812-357-
   6998 Web www.saintmeinrad.edu

Loyola University of New Orleans  6367 St. Charles Ave.
   New Orleans,La. 70118  Tel 504-864-7111  Fax 504-864-
   7247 Web www.lib.loyola.edu  Excellent collection
   of Jesuit materials

Archdiocese of Boston Archives  2121 Commonwealth
   Brighton,Mass. 02135  Tel 617-254-0100  Fax 617-
   783-5642  Extensive arcdiocesan records.

Boston College Libraries  140 Commonwealth Avenue
   Chestnut Hill,Mass  02467  Tel 617-552-3195  Fax
   617-552-8828 Web  www.bc.edu/libraries.html

St. Hyacinth College and Seminary Library  66 School St
   Granby,Mass. 01033  Tel413-467-7191  Fax 413-467-9609
   Polish Catholic material and Maximillan Kolbe Collection

Bishop Baraga Association Archives  347 Rock Street
   Marquette,Michigan 49855  Tel 906-227-9117  Fax 906-
   228-2469 Web. www.dioceseofmarquette.org

St. Mary's College  3535 Indian Trail  Orchard Lake,
   Michigan 48324  Tel 248-706-4211  Fax 248-683-4052
   Web www.mi.verio.com?smlib
   Good collection of Polish Catholic materials.

Kenrick-Glennon Seminary Library  5200 Glennon
    Dr.  St. Louis, Mo.  63119  Tel 314-792-6100
    Fax 314-792-6503  www.kenrick.edu

Seton Hall University  Walsh Library  400 S. Orange
    Ave.  So. Orange,NJ 07079  Tel 973-761-9435  Fax
    973-761-9438  www.library.shu.edu  Contains much
    diocesan historical material

Canisius College  Boowhuis Library  2001 Main Street
    Buffalo, NY  14208  Tel 716-888-2900  Fax 716-888-
    8420  Web www.canisius.edu.

Xavier University  McDonald Memorial Library  3800
    Victory Pkwy  Cincinnati,Ohio  45207  Tel 513-745-
    3884  Fax 513-745-1932  Web  www.xv.edu/library
    Special collection of Jesuit materials

Villanova University  Falvey Memorial Library  Villa-
    nova,Penna. 19085  Tel 610-519-4270  Fax 610-519-
    5018  Web  www.library.villanova.edu

Byzantine Catholic Seminary of SS Cyril and Methodius
    3605 Perrysville Ave.  Pittsburgh,Penna  15214
    Tel 412-321-8383  Fax 610-321-9936  Web.  www.
    besofi@sginet  Conatins extesnive records of
    Byzantine Catholic parishes.

St. Joseph's university  5600 City Line Ave  Philadelphia
    Penna.19131  Tel 610-660-1197  Fax 610-660-1604
    Web  www.sju.edu/libr.

Diocese of Amarillo  6800 N. Spring  Amarillo,Tex 79117
    Tel 806-383-2243  Fax 806-383-8452  Contains hist-
    orical material of the Catholic Church in the panhandle

Catholic Archives of Texas Library  16 th and Congress
    Austin,Texas 78711  Tel 512-426-6296  Fax 512-476-3715
    Web  www.onr.com/user/cat

Archdiocese of San Antonio  W. Woodlawn  San Antonio,
    Texas 78228  Tel 210-784-1609  Web  www.archdiocese.org

Catholic Diocese of Jackson  237 E. Amite St.  Jackson,
    Mississippi  39325  Tel 601-969-1880.  Archives of
    parishes in the diocese.

Catholic Diocesan Archives  1023 W. Riverside Avenue
Spokane,Wash.  99201  Tel 509-358-4293  Fax 509-
358-7302 Contain Eastern Washington Catholic
histories.

Diocese of LaCrosse Archives  P.O. Box 4004 La Crosse,
Wisconsin 54602  Tel 608-788-7700  Fax 608-788-8413
www.diocese of lacrosse.ocm

Viterbo University Library  815 S. 9th Street La Crosse,
Wisconsin 54601  Tel 608-796-3270  Fax 608-796-3275
Web www.viterbo.edu/libr

Marquette University Memorial Library  1415 W. Wisconsin
Ave.  Milwaukee,Wisconsin 53201  Tel 414-288-7210
Fax 414-288-5324  Web. www.marquette.edu/libr

Diocesan Resource Center  34 Fenner St. Providence,
Rhode Island  02903  Tel 401-278-4646  Fax 401-
278-4645  Web www.dioceseofprovidence.org

Philadelphia Archdiocese Historical Research
Center  100 E. Wynnewood Road  Wynnewood,
Pennsylvania 19096  Tel 610-667-2125  Fax
610-667-2730  Web www.rcnet/philadelphia/
pahrc/index.html

## SALVATION ARMY

William Booth was a Methodist minister in England in the 1860s who
left the ministry of that church to work with the poverty-stricken
of London. He received little support from established churches in
working with the poor and therefore established his own church
using military terms (Articles of War) to describe his work in
saving souls. The work spread quickly over England, Scotland, and
Wales and eventually throughout Europe and to the United States.
Today the Salvation Army is working in 82 countries using some
25,000 officers preaching in 111 languages and operating more than
3,000 social institutions. General membership in the United States
is estimated at 500,000.

Salvation Army Archives   120 W. 14th St.   New York, New York 10011

# SCHWENKFELDER

This group was named afetr Caspar Schwenkfeld
von Ossig who attempted reforms in the 16th century German church. A group of his followers came
to America in 1734 and formed a society of Schwenk-
felders in 1782. Today the denomination consists
of 5 congregations with a menbership of 2,200, all
of which are in a 50-mile radius of Philadelphia.

Schwenkfelder Library  105 Seminary Ave. Pennsburg,
   Pennsylvania  18073  Tel 215-679-3103 . Fax 215-
   679-8175  Web  www.Schwenkfelder.com  Maintains
   a collection of Schwenkfelder history and theology.

## SHAKERS

Shakers is the name applied to the "United Society of Believers in Christ's Second Appearing," a group first developing in America in 1774 at Watervliet, New York. It flourished until about 1860 and then began to diminish. Today there are only a few remaining members in New Hampshire and Maine.

Shaker Village at Pleasant Hill  3501 Lexington Road  Harrodsburg, Kentucky 40330. Tel 859-734-5411  Fax 859-734-7278  Web www.shakervillage ky.org  Has records covering period 1783-1865

Shaker Library  707 Shaker Road  New Gloucester, Maine 04260  Tel 207-926-4865  Fax 207-926-4597 Web www.shaker.me.us/library  Records back to 1782

Elkins Public Library  9 Center Road  Canterbury, New Hampshire 03224  Tel 603-783-4386  Fax 603-783-4817  Web www.elkinspubliclibrary.org Records from 1783

Shaker Museum  88 Museum Road  Old Chatham, New York 12136  Tel 518-794-9100  Fax 518-794-8621  Web www.shakermuseumandlibrary.org  Records range from 1865 to 1918

Western Reserve Historical Society  10825 East Blvd. Cleveland, Ohio  44106  Tel 216-721-5722  Fax 216-721-0891  Web www.wrhs.org  Shaker records going back to the 1780s.

Shaker Heights Public Library  16500 Van Aken Blvd. Shaker Heights, Ohio  44120  Tel 216-991-2040 Fax 216-991-5951  Web www.shakerlibrary.org

South Union Shaker Village  Julia Neal Museum Library 850 Shaker Museum Rd  Auburn, Kentucky  42206 Tel 270-542-4167

## SWEDENBORGIAN

Also known as the Church of New Jerusalem this
group was named after the Swedish scientist-
clergyman, Emmanuel Swedenborg, who claimed spec-
ial revelation through communication with the
other world. There are three main bodies of
Swedenborgians in America with about 20,000
members.

Urbana University  Swedenborg Memorial Library
    579 College Way  Urbana, Ohio  43078  Tel
    937-484-1335  Fax  937-653-8551  Web. www.
    urbana.edu  A college operated by the Swed-
    enborgians

Bryn Athyn College  Swedenborg Library  2925
    Gollege Drive  Bryn Athyn, Pennsylvania 19009
    Tel 267-502-2547  Fax 267-502-2637  Web  www.
    brynathyn.edu/library  Contains the national
    archives of the denomination

Swedenborgian Library and Archives  1798 Scenic
    Avenue  Berkeley, California  94709  Tel 510-
    849-8248  Fax 510-849-8296  Web  www.sh.psr.edu

Swedenborg School of Religion Library  1320 Center
    Street  Newton Center, Massachusetts  02159
    Tel  627-244-0504  Web  www.ssr.com
    Archives of Swedenborgian churches.

# UNITARIAN UNIVERSALIST

This denomination is a merger of two previously-existing groups with comparable beliefs. Its roots are in 17th century England and early American organization took place in Philadelphia in 1790. While differing with historic Christian doctrine it seeks unity among all religions. Headquarters are in Boston. There are about 200,000 members in 1,000 churches.

Starr King School for the Ministry 2441 Le Conte Berkeley, Caifornia 94709 Tel 510-845-6232 Fax 510-845-6273

All Souls Unitarian Church 5805 E. 56th Street Indianapolis, Indiana 46226 Web www.iserve. net/allsouls Has local Unitarian history

Meadville Lombard Theological Seminary 5701 S. Woodlawn Ave Chicago, Illinois 60637 Tel 773-266-3000 Fax 773-266-3007 Web www.meadville. edu

Unitarian Universalist Archives 25 Beacon Street Boston, Massachusetts 02108 Tel 617-742-2100 Fax 617-948-6114 Web www.uua.org National repository for Unitarian-Universalist archives

Andover-Harvard Theological Seminary 45 Francis Ave. Cambridge, Massachusetts 02138 Tel 617-495-5788 Fax 617-496-4111 Has records dating back to 1716

# UNITED CHURCH OF CHRIST

This denomination represents a bringing together of
the traditions of four previous groups; the Congregational Church, the Christian Church, the Evangelical
Synod and the Reformed Church, the first two being
English in background and other two, German. In 1959
the United Church of Christ was formally organized
at Oberlin, Ohio. Today there are about two million
members in 7,000 congregations.

United Church of Christ Connecticut Conference Arch-
    ives 125 Sherman Street  Hartford, Conn. 06105.
    Tel 860-233-5564  Fax 860-231-8111  Web www.
    ctucc.org

Hartford Theological Seminary  77 Sherman Street
    Hartford, Connecticut  06105  Tel 860-509-9500
    Fax  860-509-9509  Eeb www.library.hartford
    sem.edu

Divinity Library  Yale University  409 Prospect St.
    New Haven, Connecticut o6511  Tel 203-432-5274
    Fax 203-432-3906  Web www.library.yale.edu/div

Chicago Theological Seminary Library  5757 University
    Avenue  Chicago, Illinois 60637  Tel 773-322-0225
    Fax 773-752-7194  Web www.ctschicago.edu

Washburn University  1700 SW College Avenue  Wash-
    burn, Kansas 66621  Tel 785-670-1485  Fax 785-670-
    3223  Web www.washburn.edu/mabee

Bangor Theological Seminary  2 College Circle  Bangor,
    Maine 04402  Tel 207-942-6781 · Fax  207-874-2214
    Web www.bts.edu/library  Associated with the old
    Congregational Church

Divinity School Library  Harvard University  45 Francis
    Avenue  Cambridge, Massachusetts 02138  Tel 617-495-
    7738  Fax  617-496-4111  Web www.hds.harvard.edu/
    library

Congregational Christian Historical Society  14
   Beacon St.. Boston,Massachusetts  02108  Tel
   617-523-0470   Contains archives of one of
   the predecessor bodies

Webster University  101 Edgar.' Road  St. Louis,
   Missouri  Tel 314-968-6952 ' Fax 314-968-6950
   Web  www.webster.edu  Has records of the old
   Reformed Church

Doane College Perkins Library  1014 Boswell Ave.
   Crete,Nebraska  68333  Tel 402-826-8565.· Fax
   402-826-8199 ' Web  www.doane.edu  Has a
   United Church of Christ historical collection

Evangelical and Reformed Historical Society  555
   W. James  Lancaster,Pennsylvania  17603  Tel
   717-290-8734  Fax  717-735-8157  Web  www.
   erh.info Extensive records of the former
   Evangelical and Reformed Church

# WESLEYAN

The Wesleyan Churches have roots back to 1843 amid a
time of protest against both slavery and the Methodist
espiscopacy. In its early years the group was known as
the Wesleyan Methodist Church until 1968 when it merged
with the Pilgrim Holiness Church and changed the name
to simply, the Wesleyan Church. This church along with
another group called the Wesleyan Holiness Association
of Churches,is close in doctrine to both the Church of
the Nazarene and to Methodism with a time-honored
teaching of sanctification. There are about 100,000
members in 1,700 congregations.


Asbury Theological Seminary - 204 N. Lexington Avenue
    Wilmore,Kentucky 40390   Tel 859-859-2229   Fax 859-
    858-2350  Web  Asburyseminary.edu  Has many Wesley-
    an Holiness historical papers.

Bartlesville Wesleyan College  2201 Silver Lake Road
    Bartlesville,Oklahoma  74006  Tel 918-335-6285
    Fax 918-335-6220  Web  www.bwc.edu

Houghton College Memorial Library One Willard Avenue
    Houghton,New York  14744  Tel 716-567-9242  Fax
    716-567-9248  Web  www.houghton.edu/library


Southern Wesleyan University Library  916 Wesleyan
    Drive  Central,South Carolina 29630  Tel 864-644-
    5060  Fax 864-644-5900  Web www.swu.edu/library
    Records of Wesleyan churches in the south

Wesleyan Historical Center State Road 37  Marion College
    MarionIndiana  46952  Tel  765-677-2184  Fax 765-677-
    2767 Web  www.indwes.edu/library  Has national arc-
    hives of the Wesleyan Church dating back to 1783.

Vennard College  2300 8th Ave. University Park,Iowa 52595
    Tel 641-673-4345  Fax 641-673-8365 Web  www.vennard.edu/
    library  Contains Wesleyan Holiness records.

# BIBLIOGRAPHIC RESOURCES

Gaustad,E. & Barlow P.   New Historical Atlas
   of Religions in America   New York: Oxford
   University Press   2000

Mead,Frank   Handbook of Denominations   Nashville: Abingdon Press .2011

Melton. J.G.   Encyclopedia of American Religions   Detroit: Gale Research   1999

The American Library Directory   New Providence
   New Jersey: Bowker   2012

Yearbook of American and Canadian Churches
   Nashville: Abingdon Press   2012

www.ingramcontent.com/pod-product-compliance
Lightning Source LLC
LaVergne TN
LVHW021623080426
835510LV00019B/2738